SCHMEGOOGLE

YIDDISH WORDS FOR MODERN TIMES

DANIEL KLEIN

CHRONICLE BOOKS
SAN FRANCISCO

Library of Congress Cataloging-in-Publication Data available.

ISBN 978-1-7972-0727-8

Manufactured in China.

MIX
Paper from responsible sources
FSC
www.fsc.org
FSC™ C008047

Design by **Cat Grishaver**.

10 9 8 7 6 5 4 3 2 1

Chronicle Books LLC
680 Second Street
San Francisco, California 94107
www.chroniclebooks.com

CONTENTS

INTRODUCTION

IT'S THE PERFECT TIME TO BRING YIDDISH UP TO DATE.

That colorful language that sings with poetry, irony, and wit, that supplies English slang with indispensable words like *schlep* and *gnosh*, is ripe for a twenty-first century upgrade. For new words that speak to the world of online dating, social media, blended families, marijuana aficionados, and more.

Here to the rescue are new Yiddish words like *cyber-schmooze* and *faceboopkes*, *transmitzvah*, *baruch-a-toke*, and *gnoshaholic*, and, of course, *schmegoogle*—scores of newly minted terms and phrases for an up-to-date and vibrant Yiddish that will once again enrich English and describe life as we live it today.

So hang on to your *tucheses* and dive into this one-of-a-kind dictionary of a newborn lingo.

1

SOCIAL MEDIA AND TECHNOLOGY

cyberschmooze

v. **To engage in long, animated, and gossipy conversation on the internet.**

"Mildred has transitioned smoothly from the neighborhood gossip to the consummate Facebook gossip. She has turned **cyberschmoozing** into an art form."

Since the beginning of the Diaspora, Jews have had to adapt to new cultures and languages, including the creation of a "secret" language for communication among themselves: Yiddish itself. **Cyberschmoozing** is just the latest step.

From the Yiddish **schmooze**, to talk intimately and cozily; also, to gossip. A **cyberschmooze** vocabulary is absolutely necessary in contemporary Yiddish for the simple reason that Jews yak a lot, always have, and now continue to do so in cyberspace.

schmegoogle

n. **A person who is so insignificant that when you Google their name, nothing comes up.**

"Morty, God bless him, never married, only goes out of the house to work in the grocery stock room, and never joined a club, political party, or synagogue. On top of it all, he doesn't own a computer or cell phone. No wonder nobody ever heard of him. He's a bona fide **schmegoogle**."

The full impact of this put-down is understood when you try this simple experiment: Type an outlandish name into Google and watch a multitude of entries appear. And this **schmegoogle** only gets a "Your search did not match any documents"? Oy, such a **draycup** (loser).

Schmegoogle is derived from a long list of Yiddish put-down words that begin with *sch*, such as **schmo**, **schmuck**, **schmendrick**, **schlemiel**, and **schlimazel**, to name but a few. Old Yiddish dictionaries tell us that a **schlemiel** is a clumsy person and a **schlimazel** is a very unlucky person; to wit, a **schlemiel** is somebody who often spills his soup and a **schlimazel** is the person it lands on. Note: **Schmegoogle** is not always a pejorative. In the Talmud, the person who does good deeds while making sure that no one knows about it or who he is, is considered a moral prince.

faceboopkes

n. **Facebook posts of trivial and/or boring content.**

"All he writes about on Facebook is what he had for breakfast—total **faceboopkes**."

Faceboopkes is derived from the Yiddish word **boopkes** or **bupkes**, meaning trivial, a ridiculously small amount, or absolutely nothing at all; as in, "So I hired this fancy new tax accountant, but what did he save me? **Bupkes**!" **Bupkes** came into Yiddish from Polish, in which it means goat or horse droppings, though goat droppings actually are worth something if you are in the fertilizer business.

faceshtick

n. **A humorous post on Facebook, usually to garner "likes" from Facebook friends.**

"Aaron posted the old Henny Youngman 'Take my wife' routine for his morning Facebook entry. That **faceshtick** is so old and backward, the last time I heard it I fell off my dinosaur."

Granted it is hard to be truly funny these days when everyone fancies themselves a stand-up comic, but the sorry state of many of these humorous posts is mind-boggling. Almost as mind-boggling as the number of people who feel compelled to click on "like."

From the Yiddish **shtick**, meaning a funny routine or gimmick. As in this **faceshtick** thigh-slapper: "I had soy bacon for breakfast. Oy, what I do for my mother!"

tweetzpah

adj. **Quality of a person whose tweets are over-the-top and self-serving.**

"Mickey just tweeted that he is only one vote short of winning this year's Nobel Prize in economics. The man can't even balance his checkbook. It's just more of Mickey's **tweetzpah**."

The German philosopher Friedrich Nietzsche said, "All I need is a sheet of paper and something to write with, and then I can turn the world upside down." Imagine the world's gyrations if the famously self-involved iconoclast had been able to tweet. **Tweetzpah**!

Derived from the Yiddish **chutzpah**, meaning arrogance, brazenness, presumptuousness.

instaglitsh

n. **Mistakenly posting the wrong photo on Instagram.**

"Selma posted a photo of her boyfriend, Vinny, writing his name in the snow with his urine, when she really meant to post a snap of him making latkes. An epic **instaglitsh**!"

How often this happens makes the head spin. Of course, Freud says we never really make mistakes—it's our unconscious expressing itself.

Derived from the Yiddish **glitsh** (Americanized as *glitch*), meaning slip or nosedive.

instaschmutz

n. **Dirty pictures posted purposely on Instagram, often of oneself.**

"Anthony did it again—posted another sleazy selfie on Instagram. He's out of control. The man is the **mlkh** (king) of **instaschmutz**."

The net has made exhibitionism a breeze. But who wants to look at some **schmuck**'s **schmuck**?

Derived from the Yiddish **schmootz** or **schmutz**, meaning dirt or dirty stuff.

instaputz

n. **Someone who posts *instaschmutz*.**

"What kind of **instaputz** would post this kind of **instaschmutz**? Such a **schmo** (jerk)."

Putz comes from Yiddish, meaning a fool, but literally means a penis by way of German, where it's translated as "an adornment." Some adornment, eh? Maybe with a diamond stud. Another Yiddish penis word, **schmuck**, also means a fool or bad person. Yiddish really has it in for penises or, as some would say, idiots.

instaschmeichlers

n. **Instagram chatterers who will reply to every single post an influencer makes to win attention from their favorite celebrity.**

"Gladys just commented 'OMG, you are sooo horny' on that picture of Lizzo doing goat yoga. Gladys has become such an **instaschmeichler**."

From the Yiddish **schmeichler**, meaning an insincere flatterer.

e-chazerai

n. **Accumulated unanswered emails.**

"My inbox just maxed out with fifty starred messages. Even Gmail thinks I've got too much **e-chazerai**."

Most people are ambivalent about their **e-chazerai**. On the one hand, it adds to their overall anxiety about falling behind schedule. On the other, it makes them feel popular. Note: Not all **e-chazerai** is technically junk mail or spam. For example, those daily weather reports your mother sends you from Miami.

Chazerai, Yiddish for garbage, literally means pig stuff. In addition to penises, Yiddish is really into pigs.

e-chazerai-schmerz

n. **Anxiety over the number of accumulated unanswered emails in your inbox.**

"My **kishkas** (intestines) are in a tumult from all those emails piling up. It makes me feel like a failure. Oy, have I got **e-chazerai-schmerz**!"

See page 19 on overall anxiety about falling behind schedule. Listen to your Bubba: "**Langzamer** (slow down) already."

From the Yiddish **chazerai**, meaning a mess, and the Yiddish **schmerz**, meaning pain, often emotional or existential pain, as in **weltschmerz**, Yiddish/German for world weariness.

schnorrwebber

n. **A person who solicits funds for personal projects on the internet, such as on GoFundMe and Kickstarter. This term is deprecatory, implying that begging is begging no matter how fancy you are about it.**

"Oy, now Aunt Mitzi is on GoFundMe begging for startup money for her Museum of My Cats. And the thing is, she really will get the money. She does every time, such a **schnorrwebber** she is."

Derived from the Yiddish **schnorrer**, meaning beggar or sponger.

shmodom

n. **The status achieved by a dull person whose YouTube video, tweet, or Instagram post goes viral.**

"Chester has been strutting around like a movie star ever since his yodeled version of "Shake It Off" went viral. That's **shmodom** for ya."

Derived from the Yiddish **shmo**, meaning a dull and stupid person.

Purimshpieler's revenge

n. **When a *shmo* achieves *shmodom*.**

"We never thought Chester would amount to much, but with that viral yodeling video, he has reached the pinnacle of shmodom, his very own **Purimshpieler's revenge**."

In the late twentieth century, pop artist Andy Warhol famously said, "In the future, everyone will be world-famous for fifteen minutes." His prediction preceded the internet by decades. Such a **nbia** (prophet) was this Andy.

From the Yiddish **Purimshpieler**, meaning a rank amateur and untalented entertainer. The word **shpieler** is Yiddish for a glib speaker. **Purimshpieler** is derived from the skits, complete with songs and dances, that are performed on the holiday Purim, and the events in the book of Esther. These **shpiels** go back to the fifteenth century and, over the years, have become increasingly **nudne** (tedious).

handle hondel

v. **To trade one's online username for a new, snazzier handle; often for a stage name.**

"Once TStone's album dropped, everyone was tweeting about her, but she'll always be Toni Steiner to us."

Often the idea behind a **handle hondel** was to bleach an ethnic name so it sounded Waspy, but just as often it was simply to become snappier and more memorable. YouTube star Felix Kjellberg hondeled his name for the handle PewDiePie, and rapper James Todd Smith hondeled his for LLCool J. Of course, there's nothing new about changing one's name, especially in show biz. Tony Curtis was born Bernard Schwartz, Cary Grant was once Archibald Alec Leach, and even Norma Jeane Mortenson **hondeled her handle** into Marilyn Monroe.

From the Yiddish **hondel**, meaning to trade or bargain.

punimetrics

n. **Facial recognition technology used by both merchandisers to target potential customers, and by law enforcement officers to identify suspicious individuals.**

"Misha has such a **fakakta** (ridiculous) face, you don't need **punimetrics** to pick him out of a crowd."

While the technology has both critics and advocates, the good news about **punimetrics** is that it proves conclusively that not all Jews look alike.

From the Yiddish **punim**, meaning face and facial expressions.

electroshvindl

n. **The act of being duped and cheated by a financial transaction on the internet.**

"Poor Aunt Ruthy. The first time she made an order online, she was a victim of **electroshvindl**."

This one is no joke, as anyone who has ordered $15 gloves from an internet retailer and had their credit card charged an additional $45 for shipping and handling will attest.

From the Yiddish **shvindl**, meaning scam.

AN ONOMATOPOEIA-LOVER'S DELIGHT

Yiddish is overflowing with onomatopoetic words—words that sound like the thing or action they describe. In English, for example, the word *buzz* sounds like something that is buzzing. Ditto for *hiss*, *clippety-clop*, and *cock-a-doodle-doo*, although roosters appear to crow different songs in different languages. In French, they sing out, "Couqlacoo." Go figure.

But back to Yiddish. Take the word **blech** (an expression of disgust). It is no coincidence that it sounds like a nauseous person's gag reflex, because that is exactly what it means and where it came from.

Then there's the Yiddish slang word from the world of boxing, **klung**, which describes a punch in the teeth so powerful that the recipient hears bells ringing, *klung, klung*.

And, of course, there's the all-time favorite, **futz**, which means to fool around producing nothing of value. It's the word's origin that gives us the onomatopoeia—**futz** came from the expression **arumfartsn zikh**, literally meaning to fart around. Yup, we can hear that.

amazhlub

n. **Those whose entire lives—from what they purchase to what they watch—is provided by Amazon.com.**

"Milty thinks he lives in the United States of Amazon, such an **amazhlub** he is. Once they get their drones dropping down his orders on his porch, he'll never have to leave the house."

Some estimates put **amazhlubs** at 50 percent of the USpopulation.

From the Yiddish **zhlub**, meaning a simpleton.

uber menschlich

n. **An Uber driver who turns out to be courteous and helpful.**

"Alona's Uber driver was such an **uber menschlich**, he carried her shopping bag to her front door."

Such a happy occurrence this is, although with a shadowy history. **Uber menschlich** comes to us by way of the Nietzschean term *ubermensch*, meaning superman, a man superior to ordinary human beings. The concept was, of course, taken up by Aryan supremacists. One does wonder what the independent chauffeuring company had in mind when they chose this moniker.

From the German *über*, meaning a superlative example of its kind, and from the Yiddish **menschlich**, meaning human.

netfermischt

adj. **The mental state of a person who has watched so many assorted series on streaming platforms that they confuse the characters and plot turns of one series with the characters and plot turns in another.**

"Dina is so **netfermischt**, she thinks Mrs. Maisel is having an affair with Prince Charles in *The Crown*."

There have been cases when people afflicted with a case of **netfermischt** find that their entire waking lives suffer from the same confusion, as in, "Was it Sylvia who left her husband or was it Sophie? I'm having trouble keeping track."

From the Yiddish **fermischt**, meaning mixed up in the head.

so nu? app

n. **The absolutely latest app. Install it and find out immediately how your closest friends are doing.**

"Lila is so connected, she installs another **so nu? app** every ten minutes."

If this app domain name hasn't been purchased yet, somebody do it quick. Just cut me in.

From the common Yiddish expression **So nu?**, meaning, among many, many other things, "Wassup?"

niche shadkn

n. **A web-based matchmaking service that narrows down its clientele to a very small and selective group.**

"Nadia is so picky about whom she dates, she joined a **niche shadkn** called J/2 BLT for half-Jews who enjoy eating bacon."

For instance, Red Yenta, a dating site for socialist and communist singles. (True.) Who ever thought that making a **shidduch** (marriage match), once the enterprise of the village's wise old **yenta** (busybody), would be taken over by algorithms?

From the Yiddish **shadkn**, meaning matchmaker.

mini-megillah

n. **A post on social media that is too long to keep its reader's attention, like a Twitter thread that just goes on and on.**

"My eyes glazed over when I read Asher's five-paragraph Facebook entry about his dinner at Olive Garden. Such a **mini-megillah** it was."

This new term acknowledges the new, abbreviated attention span.

From the Yiddish **megillah**, meaning an interminable and tedious story.

begoogled oysshteler

n. **A self-aggrandizing loudmouth who is easily debunked by a five-second Google search.**

"What a **begoogled oysshteler**! He thinks he can say he graduated from Princeton and dated Dolly Parton and nobody's going to check him out on the web?"

Gone are the days when a person could tell whoppers about himself without fear of being exposed as a fraud. This is undoubtedly Google's greatest contribution to modern culture.

From the Yiddish **oysshteler**, meaning a braggart and egotist.

schmelinkedin

n. **Someone who consults the job posting website LinkedIn several times daily, each time convinced that this is the time they will find the job of their dreams—yet they never find it.**

"Poor Ethan, he hates his job so much that he's become a **schmelinkedin**."

Yes, another Yiddish put down, but oh-so-sad.

From the **sch-** prefix of Yiddish words of belittlement, such as **schlemiel** (clumsy) and **schlimazel** (unlucky).

hock app

n. **A phone app that reminds a person to do a task at a particular time, like BZ Reminder and Microsoft To Do.**

"Rina even has a **hock app** to remind her to set her alarm clock."

These apps not only remind you what to do and when to do it with flashing flags, whistles, and beeps emanating from your phone, but they also continue to nag you until the task is done. Some people find this self-inflicted discipline annoying and long for the good old days when a parent or spouse did the hocking.

From the Yiddish **hock**, to bother or nag incessantly, as in **hockn my chinik** (to knock a teakettle), apparently a noisy and annoying business.

schmutz app

n. **An app that delivers pornographic content.**

"So I've got a **schmutz app** on my phone. Big deal. What, you don't?"

To put things in perspective, internet traffic analysts note that the two most accessed porn sites are more popular than Twitter, eBay, and Netflix. **Azoy zeyn es** (roughly, "It is what it is").

From the Yiddish, **schmutz**, meaning dirt or dirty stuff.

bubbe maiseh-trap

n. **An untrue story that captures one's mind; known in the media as "faux" news.**

"According to Melvin's latest tweet, Martians are putting drugs in our toothpaste. Of course, Melvin gets all his **bubbe maiseh-traps** from a website run by certifiable nutcases."

From the Yiddish **bubbe maiseh**, literally a grandmother's tale, a fanciful story.

online-in-aroys

adj. **The personality characteristic of someone who is more open and honest about themself on social media than they are face-to-face.**

"I know more about Lucy's love life from her Twitter than from sitting next to her on the bus every day. You know, she's one of those **online-in-aroys** types."

From the Yiddish **in aroys**, meaning inside out.

2

FAMILY

klutz clan

n. **A family whose members are all clumsy.**

"Did you see there's another Finkelstein with a sprained ankle? Such a **klutz clan** are those Finkelsteins."

From the Yiddish **klutz**, meaning clumsy or awkward.

ivy-fashtupn

v. **Pushing one's child to get into an Ivy League college.**

"All Abby thinks about is getting her little Ezra into Yale, so it's **ivy-fashtupn** time from dawn 'til dusk."

Victims of **ivy-fashtupn** are sometimes as young as five years old, and their families apply to elite "pre-Ivy" kindergartens to the tune of $50,000 a year. All this so your kid can carry a six-figure college loan well into middle age.

Directly from the Yiddish **fashtupn**, meaning to push or shove.

ivy-fardeiget

n. **Anxiety over pressure to get into an Ivy League college.**

"Morty has such a case of **ivy-fardeiget** that he thinks he is already on the brink of failure at the age of fifteen."

Note: In five-year-olds, this phenomenon is known as **early-onset fardeiget**.

Fardeiget is Yiddish for angst.

bare mitzvah

n. **A Jewish gender reveal party at which expectant parents reveal the gender of their gestating child, usually by using items, like cake frosting or balloons, that are either pink or blue. Sometimes the party includes a projection of an ultrasound photo of the fetus, naked, of course. So cute.**

"Sam and Suzie's **bare mitzvah** was a big hit. Everybody raised their beer bottles when they saw the ultrasound."

From the Yiddish, **bar/bat mitzvah**, meaning the coming-of-age ritual and celebration of a twelve- year-old female or thirteen-year-old male.

transmitzvah

n. **The bar/bat mitzvah of a transgender thirteen-year-old.**

"Join us for the **transmitzvah** of our daughter Penny (née Peter) Goldstein, followed by a party featuring her favorite performance artist, Sour Pickles."

From the term *trans*, short for *transgender*, meaning someone who does not identify with the gender they were assigned at birth.

cismitzvah

n. **The bar/bat mitzvah of a cisgender thirteen-year-old.**

"Join us for the **cismitzvah** of our son Bob ("Bucky") Bernstein, followed by a party featuring his favorite rapper, T-Reg."

From the term *cis*, an abbreviation of *cisgender*, meaning someone who identifies with the gender they were assigned at birth.

b-mitzvah

n. **A gender-neutral bar/bat mitzvah for a nonbinary thirteen-year-old who does not identify as a boy or girl.**

"Join us for the **b-mitzvah** of our child, Skyler Cohen. Please, no neckties or hairpins for presents, but Skyler would be happy if you gave them a subscription to *Game Informer*."

Some Jewish communities are already addressing this issue with a variety of other neologisms, like the gender-neutral **b'nai mitzvah**. Also, **zera mitzvah** (seed/offspring of the commandment), **simchat mitzvah** (joy of the commandment), and **brit mitzvah** (covenant of the commandment). Our kiddush cup runneth over with new names.

From the Yiddish/Hebrew **bar mitzvah**.

hemitzvah

n. **The bar or bat mitzvah of a half-Jewish person.**

"They say Troy is only going to recite a half-**haftarah** (the section of the *Torah* traditionally chanted by the bar mitzvah boy or bat mitzvah girl) at his **hemitzvah**."

In fact, there is nothing "half" or "hemi" at all about the bar and bat mitzvahs of half-Jews. It's the real and whole deal. But, of course, there's always some wise guy with a half-Jewish gag, like the one about the half-Jew who only lights four candles on Hanukkah.

From the prefix *hemi-*, meaning half or bifurcated.

roamitzvah

n. **A "destination bar mitzvah," a bar or bat mitzvah celebrated in a place other than the bar mitzvah boy's/bat mitzvah girl's home synagogue.**

"Adam's **roamitzvah** is being held at Hotel Riu Palace Riviera Maya in Mexico. They're flying in a kosher chef."

For some families, this means at the Wailing Wall in Jerusalem, for others it means the Fontainebleau Hotel in Miami Beach. What's next—destination funerals? Already happening, according to Co-op Funeral-care. Does this mean sitting **shiva** (ritual Jewish mourning period) in the lobby of the Hôtel Barrière Le Majestic in Cannes? Wearing black bathing suits, we trust.

From the English *roam*, and the Hebrew/Yiddish **bar/bat mitzvah**.

black mitzvah

n. **The bar or bat mitzvah of an African American Jew.**

"Talia played a whole Sammy Davis Jr. medley at her **black mitzvah**."

Some Africans and African Americans are Members of the Tribe and many have been for millennia. There are several African American synagogues in America, including Beth Shalom B'nai Zaken Ethiopian Hebrew Congregation in Chicago, whose chief rabbi, Capers Funnye, is a cousin of Michelle Obama.

The term **Black mitzvah** was coined by award-winning actor and comedian Tiffany Haddish, who celebrated her **black mitzvah**, at the age of forty, in a Netflix special. Haddish's father is an Eritrean Jew.

IRONY: THE YIDDISH WORLDVIEW

If you inhabit a world with fifty different kinds of snow, your language will contain fifty different words for snow and you will perceive the difference between each kind. Similarly, if your culture's belief system sees something divine in every object, your language will probably reflect that, perhaps with a prefix that makes the word for table into "God's table."

People in Yiddish culture are certainly programmed to **kvetch** (complain)—the language is loaded to the gills with words and phrases of complaint, starting with the most popular Yiddish expression, **Oy!** Followed by scores more, ranging from **chaloshes** (disgusting) to **ungebloozen** (pouty). **Kvetch, kvetch**, whine, whine. It's a regular way of life.

But what's this? Yiddish is also chock-full of words of endearment. People routinely greet friends and neighbors with **zei azoy gut**, which means be so good. And invariably after someone thanks you, the Yiddish response is **nisht do kein farvos** (there is no why), sincerely denying that there is any reason for the thanks.

So exactly what kind of worldview do Yiddish speakers have? Both caustic and warm? There's something ironic about that.

And that turns out to be the key to the Yiddish worldview: irony! The friction between a wearisome world and the indomitable will to survive it. Hey, it's all a cosmic joke, so let's keep laughing.

demigoy

***n.* A person who is half-Jewish.**

"Hey, I'm not only half-Jewish, I'm also half–Native American. I'm a **demigoy**."

This new term supplies full acknowledgment to one's non-Jewish half. Note that currently in the United States, there are as many half-Jews as full-Jews. Some identify as Jewish, some do not. So it goes.

From the Yiddish **goy**, meaning a gentile. This, in turn, derives from the Hebrew word for nation, implying that Jews were not a part of the nation in which they lived, just as the Jews who lived in the **shtetls** of Eastern Europe were not considered Polish or Russian, etc.

matzah-pizza

***n.* A subgroup of *demigoys* who are half-Jewish and half-Italian.**

"Leah Cristaldi says **oy veh** when she's upset and *fuhgeddaboudit* when she's not. A classic **matzah-pizza**."

This one is to smile, especially with these blended kids bearing such names as Rocco Finestein and Adina Bonavitacola.

Matzah-pizza was coined in Massapequa, Long Island, where this mix is common. (True.) **Matzah-pizza** sounds like "Massapequa" to the people of Massapequa.

cashew

n. **A subgroup of *demigoys* who are half-Jewish and half-Catholic.**

"Chris's brother is a Jesuit monk and his sister belongs to Hadassah. It's your regular **cashew** family."

The comedian Bill Maher, who is a **cashew**, has a famous **shtick** based on his **demigoyness**, which includes the line, "When I went to confession, I brought a lawyer with me. Bless me, father, for I have sinned. . . . I believe you know Mr. Cohen." **Cashews** have a long history in America, dating back to the immigrant wave of Jews and Irish Catholics who came to New York City in the early 20th century. At that time, the popular Broadway comedy *Abie's Irish Rose* celebrated one such romance.

Originally, this term was **cathjew**, but the temptation to morph it to **cashew** proved irresistible.

Juslim

n. **A subgroup of *demigoys* who are half-Jewish and half-Muslim.**

"As my uncle Zack says, 'If we had more **Juslims**, all this fighting would stop already.'"

This blend was bound to happen, and not just in Jerusalem. The mix is on.

This term was introduced in a tweet about a Jewish girl named Casey and her best friend, a Muslim girl named Yasmin, who dressed up for Halloween as a superhero team, the **Juslims**. The delightful story went viral and since then, the term has been adopted by many half-Jewish, half-Muslim people.

bisselbubbe

n. **The gentile grandmother of a *demigoy*.**

"My **bisselbubbe** actually sings to herself while doing the dishes. This you would never see on the other half of my family tree."

It's tricky for all involved. The implication is that a **bisselbubbe** can never be a total **bubbe**, For that, she would have to be bossy, generous, sentimental, and prone to guilt-mongering. The difference between a gentile grandmother and a Jewish grandmother is illustrated in this classic "gentile joke" told by Jews: A gentile grandson phones his gentile grandmother and says, "I'm sorry, Grams, but I have to cancel our dinner tonight. Instead, I'm going to watch football on TV with my friends." Gentile grandmother: "No problem, Chris. Have a wonderful time with your friends." A **bubbe** she is not.

Derived from the Yiddish **bissel** (or **bisl**) meaning a little bit, and **bubbe**, meaning grandmother. Combined, they mean a little bit a grandmother or not quite a grandmother, but close.

ersatzayde

n. **The gentile grandfather of a *demigoy*.**

"My **ersatzayde** will do anything to win over his **demigoy** grandkids. He peppers his conversations with Yiddish words like **chutzpah**, which he pronounces 'hoots-paw.' It's the effort that counts."

Derived from the Yiddish **zayde**, meaning grandfather, and **ersatz**, meaning a substitute for something else.

Chrismukkah

n. **The combined celebration of Christmas and Hanukkah observed by mixed-faith families.**

"This year's office **Chrismukkah** party is being catered by Sam's Deli and Mrs. Spence's Bakery."

The holidays come at around the same time of year, and both involve songs, presents, good food, and good cheer. This combo is a natural.

The term entered English big time in 2003 when it was part of the popular TV drama *The O.C.*

Mogen David dingle-dangle

n. **A Jewish, six-pointed star as an ornament on a Christmas tree in a mixed-faith home. Such trees are sometimes known as Hanukkah bushes.**

"Should we put the **Mogen David dingle-dangle** next to the elf dingle-dangle or the manger dingle-dangle?"

For some, the **Mogen David dingle-dangle** on the **Chrismukkah** tree is a step too far in cultural amalgamation in light of the Mogen David armbands of the Nazi era. The six-pointed star as a symbol of Jewry dates back to David's hexagram-shaped shield in the book of Samuel in the Old Testament. **Mogen** is ancient Hebrew for shield. Mogen David is also the name of a Chicago winery that produces the sweet wine imbibed at Passover Seders. It's an acquired taste.

Rebbe Krazy Katz

n. **A mythical feline who knows the Talmud inside and out, like a yarn of wool; often mews holy prayers.**

"Poor old Zackary, he's been living alone so long he actually thinks **Rebbe Krazy Katz** is sitting on his lap, listening to him sing."

Belief that one's cats not only possess Talmudic wisdom, but can somehow vocalize it, is more prevalent than one would expect, especially by the elderly who live alone. Hey, if it works for them. In any event, it's no harder to swallow than a burning bush that intones eternal truths.

From the Yiddish **katz**, meaning cats.

Yiddishe pooch

n. **A dog who has learned and responds to commands in Yiddish.**

"Daisy is a **Yiddishe pooch**. Tell her to go **kibbitz** (make wisecracks and give advice), and she chews the other dogs' ears off. Not literally, of course."

Yiddishe pooches are for real; New Yorkers can even attend Yiddish dog training seminars in Central Park.

Yiddishe means Jewish.

machatunausea

n. **The feeling of revulsion one feels at having to spend time with the parents of your child's spouse's parents.**

"Oy, here comes the big family Thanksgiving dinner, with our Mel's in-laws. I feel **machatunausea** coming on."

From the Yiddish **machatunim**, for the parents of your son- or daughter-in-law. Yiddish is one of the few Western languages to name this relationship. Romanian is another.

finster pisher

n. **A gloomy young child who often breaks their parents' hearts with their dolefulness.**

"Little Melvin doesn't whine or cry. He just sits there looking forsaken all the time. Such a **finster pisher**."

We've been hearing a lot about such kids lately. It really is heartbreaking.

From the Yiddish-via-German **finster**, meaning dark and despondent. And from the Yiddish **pisher**, literally meaning pisser, but metaphorically meaning little squirt.

3
DATING AND ROMANCE

fartshepen romantic

n. **A person who falls head-over-heels in love with several people each day.**

"Such a **fartshepen** romantic Sadie is, she fell in love with three guys named Matthew just yesterday."

Fartshepen romantics are definitely on the rise, possibly as a result of all the prospective mates one meets each day on social media. And daily life for **fartshepen romantics** is clearly more intense, but it also means more broken hearts . . . daily.

From the Yiddish **fartshepen**, meaning to get hooked.

Jewboo

n. **A Jewish girlfriend or boyfriend. This new-Yiddish term has become so popular it's already old.**

"Melvin has been my **Jewboo** for over three weeks now. It's my new record."

According to Urban Dictionary, "A one-night stand would never be classified as a **Jewboo**." The implication here is that sometimes Jewish men and women do indulge in one-night stands. What is this world coming to?

Although the slang term *boo* is sometimes used to simply mean a close friend or confidante, its most common use is for a romantic partner or lover.

J-drek

n. **A truly terrible Jdate date. Also used to describe the dregs of all Jdate candidates.**

"Oy, I caught another **J-drek** last night. One more like that and I'm joining Muslims4Marriage.com."

From the Yiddish **drek**, meaning garbage, manure, or excrement, and Jdate, an online dating service for Jewish singles.

J-chaza

n. **A guy who is not only a terrible Jdate date, but a pig.**

"On top of being **J-drek**, this guy kept trying to grab me. **J-chaza**!"

From the Yiddish **chaza**, meaning pig, which, of course, also means **traif** (unkosher). Every woman, Jewish or gentile, knows about dates who turn out to be a pigs.

J-ganif

n. **A non-Jewish person who pretends to be Jewish in order to get dates on Jdate.**

"I knew Phil was a **J-ganif** when he told me he was buying a three-piece suit for his family Seder."

A **J-ganif** claims to be a Reform Jew or a cultural Jew on Jdate. Their aim is to snag a Jewish partner, possibly because Jews are said to be more serious about marriage and family life than **goyim** (gentiles) are. In any event, **J-ganifs** are usually revealed for what they are on the first date. It is surprising how frequently this masquerade happens, but it certainly speaks well of the attractiveness of Jewish women and men.

From the Yiddish **ganif**, meaning a crook or thief.

boychik magnet

n. **A woman who attracts boyish young Jewish men.**

"Oy, this guy has the maturity of a ten-year-old. What is there about me that makes me such a **boychik magnet**?"

Let's face it, a lot of young Jewish men are boyish. It has something to do with their attachment to their mothers. On the one hand, a **boychik magnet** will get lots of marriage proposals; on the other, once married, she will take second place to the **boychik**'s mother.

Boychik is a Yiddish term of endearment for a boy or young man, as in, "You are so good to your mother, my **boychik**."

THE ROTH CONUNDRUM

In his novel *Portnoy's Complaint*, Philip Roth's protagonist tells a story of going to grade school and freezing in embarrassment in front of the class when he is asked to identify the kitchen utensil one uses to flip pancakes for breakfast. What petrifies Alexander Portnoy is the word his mother uses, *spatula*.

Was it English or Yiddish?

At home, the family mixed English and Yiddish in virtually every sentence, but God forbid he speak Yiddish in front of his classmates.

Spatula does sound Yiddish! It's that *lah* at the end that does it. As in **bubbellah** (sweetheart) or **challah** (braided egg bread).

But young Portnoy needn't have worried that *spatula* was a Yiddish word. In fact, it comes from the Latin *spatha*, meaning long sword.

Indeed, there are loads of English words that sound like they must be Yiddish or Yiddish derived, but are not. Take the word *cockamamie*. Sounds Yiddish, right? Nope, it comes to us via a convoluted word trip from French.

Ditto for *zilch*. It was adapted from a character name in an American comic strip.

The list of sounds-Yiddish-but-isn't words goes on and on.

Gibberish? Nope.

Flummoxed? No way.

Mishmash? Sorry.

Matchstick? Sorry again.

And here is the most disappointing of all—the word *svelte*. Such a lovely sound for such a lovely compliment, it just has to be Yiddish. Wrong again—it's French/Italian. *Tant pis*. (Oh well!)

Roth could have saved his narrator by letting him stammer out, "You know, she uses that . . . that pancake flipper gizmo." Of course, the problem was that *gizmo* also sounds Yiddish.

shpilksmooch

***n.* A hasty, unromantic kiss that implies that the kisser has more important things to attend to.**

"If all you've got to offer is a **shpilksmooch**, I'm better off snuggling with my dog."

People married five years or more often find they partake in more **shpilksmooches** than romantic, lip-lingering kisses. Some even forget what a romantic, lip-lingering kiss feels like.

From the Yiddish **shpilkes**, meaning impatience or having ants in one's pants.

the brirh barrier

***n.* Having too many options for first dates (via dating sites) has created the brirh barrier, an obstacle that keeps people from ever going on a gratifying date. Because daters have so many choices, they believe one of them must be the perfect match; thus, they become pickier and end up with no one.**

"**The brirh barrier** makes me yearn for the days when my choice of mates was limited to my neighborhood."

Choice-making is complicated. Look at it this way: According to the Jam Study, a famous experiment in consumer behavior, shoppers surveying twenty-four different gourmet jams were less likely to make a purchase than shoppers who looked at only six. Plus, shoppers choosing from a wider selection were unhappier with the jam they did buy. Do the math, daters.

From the Yiddish **brirh**, meaning choice.

shotgun shadkn

***n.* The unexpected child whose imminent arrival necessitates the arrangement of a marriage. In this classic situation, the child is, in effect, the *shadkn*.**

"Our little **shotgun shadkn**, Junior, arranged our marriage for us. For him, it was an act of self-interest."

From the Yiddish **shadkn** (marriage matchmaker) and the English phrase *shotgun wedding*.

shidduch envy

n. **Nostalgia for the old custom of having one's parents arrange one's marriage.**

"I miss the days when you could blame your parents for a lousy marriage choice. I have that **shidduch envy**."

From today's viewpoint, an arranged marriage is starting to look very good. Less time-consuming than the current rigmarole (see **the brirh barrier**). Fact: For a variety of reasons, arranged marriages produce significantly fewer divorces than romantically instigated marriages.

From the Yiddish **shidduch**, meaning an arranged marriage.

hiskhayves-nots

n. **People who are resistant to making a commitment in a relationship.**

"Sure, I'm a **hiskhayves-not**, but I don't fear commitment, I just fear wasting my time."

This has always been a problem, but what has changed recently is that **hiskhayves-nots** now seem to be equally distributed between women and men.

From the Yiddish **hiskhayves**, meaning commitment.

praktish linking

v. **A current trend of choosing a mate for practical reasons, such as sufficient income, agreement on desired number of children, and preferred type of home and location.**

"Romance, shmomance, life's hard enough. I'm into **praktish linking**."

This is a distinctly non-romantic type of mating, a kind of do-it-yourself **shidduch**, Yiddish for the matchmaking done by a **shadkn**, a contracted matchmaker who bases her matches on practical matters like level of learning, financial status, family, and health status.

Praktish is Yiddish for practical.

zhlub magnet

n. **A person who attracts slobs and buffoons, even via online dating services.**

"Oy, another guy who smells like five-day-old egg foo yung. How did I become such a **zhlub magnet**?"

There is something touching about **zhlub** magnets, because the source of their appeal is their openness, tolerance, and receptiveness, all sterling qualities. Unfortunately, these are also qualities that any **zhlub** can spot a mile away, even through his smudged bifocals.

From the Yiddish **zhlub** or **zhlob**, meaning a slob.

co-utz relationship

n. **A relationship based on annoying each other relentlessly; a popular form of codependency that does keep a couple from getting bored with one another.**

"Yup, Sheila and I have a **co-utz** relationship. It keeps me on my toes until they hurt, every **layzik** (lousy) one of them."

As Gilda Radner said, "Marriage is finding that special person you want to annoy for the rest of your life."

From the Yiddish **utz**, to needle or torment.

gorniship

n. **A relationship in which one party gets absolutely nothing in exchange for their love and devotion; an unequal relationship in the extreme.**

"My mother and father had a typical **gorniship**. She waited on him; he snarled at her."

A **gorniship** is a sad state of affairs, no doubt about it. Yet if it didn't exist, neither would an entire genre of poignant novels and melancholy ballads.

From the Yiddish **gornisht**, meaning zilch, nothing there. (BTW, *zilch* is one of those words that sounds Yiddish, but is not.)

brechvard tryst

n. **A romantic encounter that ends up disgusting one or both parties. It happens, like, way too often.**

"Oy, I couldn't get out of bed fast enough, such a **brechvard tryst** it turned out to be."

These encounters always raise the intensely personal question, **Ven vel ikh lernen**? (When will I learn?)

From the Yiddish **brechvard**, meaning nauseating.

kvitch switcher

n. **A person who fakes sexual satisfaction, usually to please their partner but sometimes just to get the whole business over with.**

"I could tell she was **kvitch switching** when her **kvitch** turned into a yawn."

From the Yiddish **kvitch**, meaning little yelps of pleasure.

date fermischt spreadsheet

n. **A spreadsheet listing and sorting the main characteristics of all the various people one is dating via online dating services. It is considered a perfectly rational and methodical way to conduct the business of dating, especially if you possess a disorganized mind.**

"When Hannah realized she was dating two guys named Morton and both wore steel-rimmed glasses, she knew it was time to create a **date fermischt spreadsheet**."

From the Yiddish **fermischt**, meaning mixed up in the head.

online dating chutzpah

n. **The now-prevalent practice of playing devious social media mind games with friends and lovers with the intent of keeping them in the dark about your genuine feelings. Why? you may ask. Could it be that the considerable power available to us with a few finger taps brings out the *unmensch* (lack of human decency) in us all?**

"All this **online dating chutzpah** makes me want to join a monastery. Hmm, do they take Jews?"

From the Yiddish **chutzpah**, meaning insolence or shameless audacity.

breadcrumbshpil

n. **Stringing along a friend or lover via social media just to keep your options open with minimal effort.**

"She texted me that we ought to have coffee sometime. Sometime? Sounds like a **breadcrumbshpil** to me."

From the slang term *breadcrumbing*, meaning to drop a few tantalizing crumbs of interest, and from the Yiddish **shpil**, meaning game.

catfishpil

n. **Enticing a person into a relationship by using a fictional online persona, and often including a photograph of a better-looking person instead of a photo of oneself. If this progresses to a face-to-face meeting . . . best of luck.**

"She could tell I was playing a **catfishpil** the minute she looked at me, then at my photo on her phone, then at me again. All I could say was, 'People always tell me I take a good picture.'"

From the slang term *catfishing*, as described above, and from the Yiddish **shpil**, meaning game.

kittenfishpil

n. **A dialed-down version of *catfishpil*, in which a person exaggerates personal attributes and interests in hopes of impressing a prospective date. For example, using a personal photograph that is considerably out of date, or claiming to be an avid opera aficionado, when, in fact, you don't know Renée Fleming from Bette Midler. Recommended ploy when the date discovers your deceit: Roll your eyes as if somebody else put you up to it.**

"I knew in a minute it was **kittenfishpil**, but what the hell, he had great abs."

Adapted from *catfishing*, as described on page 57, and from the Yiddish **shpil**, meaning game.

benching benching

v. **Making a prayer that your lover is not stringing you along while they keep playing the field.**

"Selma is head-over-heels in love with Teddy, but she knows he's a player. That's why she's **benching benching**."

From the modern online dating term *benching*, meaning keeping a lover on hold while they continue to pursue others. And from the Yiddish term **benching**, meaning a blessing or prayer.

oysbeyg message

n. **A supposedly caring and kindhearted online method of breaking up with a friend or lover; online rejection with a smiley face emoticon.**

"When she texted me, 'In my heart of hearts, I love you more than I actually do,' a red flag went up: **oysbeyg message**!"

It is rumored that **Yiddishe boychiks** have a special talent for **oysbeyg messaging**, having learned mixed messaging from their mothers.

From the slang *curving*, the new, compassionate way to break up online, and from the Yiddish **oysbeyg**, meaning curve.

Jewfer twofer

n. **The special romantic attraction and connection between two half-Jews.**

"It was double love at first sight. A real **Jewfer twofer**. Even my Palestinian half fell in love with her Irish half."

Think Sarah Jessica Parker and Matthew Broderick, Lisa Bonet and Lenny Kravitz, and that classic pair, writer Dorothy Parker and actor Alan Campbell. Parker called their mutual attraction "an empathy of genes."

In Yiddish, this phenomenon is called, the **topl love of tsvey halbs** (the double love of two halves). From the Yiddish **topl**, meaning double, **tsvey**, meaning two, and **halbs**, meaning halves.

farputst chazzer

n. **An unattractive person who, with the aid of a Bianca DiMillo haircut, L'Oréal cosmetics, and Gucci apparel, appears quite glamorous—at least from a discrete distance.**

"If I weren't so vain and had just put on my glasses, I would have realized she was a **farputst chazzer** before I waved her over to my table."

Hey, if it makes **farputst chazzers** feel good about themselves, why not?

From the Yiddish **farputst**, meaning made fashionable, and **chazzer**, meaning pig, contrary to the expression "You can't put lipstick on a pig."

benkshaft romance

n. **After searching the world—and multiple dating sites—for the perfect mate, finding that person in one's old neighborhood, often at a high school reunion.**

"Who would have guessed that Trudy and I would end up with one another in a **benkshaft romance**? And to think, I almost passed up the high school reunion to watch baseball in a bar!"

This seems to be happening frequently lately. Who knew? It is to **kvell** (be delighted).

From the Yiddish **benkshaft**, meaning homesickness or nostalgia.

zudikphilic

n. **A connoisseur of buttock shapes.**

"Asher calls himself a **zudikphilic**. He charts a very specific course through the museum's Greco-Roman sculpture garden."

Zudikphilics insist that there is nothing prurient about their preoccupation, comparing it to that of an art critic. Yeah, yeah.

From the Yiddish **zudik**, meaning buttocks. The suffix *-philic* (from the Greek) means an attraction or affinity for something.

vilde chaye libhober

n. **An extreme pet enthusiast who only dates other extreme pet enthusiasts.**

"Levy, that **vilde chaye libhober**, picks up women in the pit bull section of the dog run in Battery Park. They tend to be as **meshugana** (crazy) about their dogs as he is."

Vilde chaye means wild beast in Yiddish, and **libhober** means lover. To some, to describe a sex partner as a **vilde chaye** may be seen as a compliment.

4
FOOD AND WEED

meshuga-nug

n. Reefer Madness! **Someone who is just crazy about marijuana, and for whom there is no such thing as being too high.**

"Call me a **meshuga-nug**, if you will, but I think I have it all figured out. Like, *all of it*."

Meshuga-nugs often consider their preoccupation with pot as providing a rarefied form of enlightenment.

Meshuga-nug derives from the Yiddish **meshuga**, meaning crazy, and from *nug*, a choice marijuana bud containing the highest concentrations of mind-altering cannabinoids.

anti-shpilkes shpritz

n. **A colloquialism for cannabidiol (CBD) oil in a spray dispenser. CBD is a marijuana/hemp derivative sometimes used to treat anxiety.**

"Morty gets hysterical every time his son blares Lady Gaga on his speakers. Somebody spritz him with some **anti-shpilkes shpritz**."

From the Yiddish **shpilkes**, denoting nervousness and agitation, originally meaning needles, as in sitting on needles. And from the Yiddish **shpritz**, meaning to spray.

baruch-a-toke

n. **The new kiddush when substituting pot for Manischewitz wine.**

"**Baruch-a-toke?** Really? This makes me yearn for the old Talmudic debates about whether or not traditions are changing too fast."

From the Hebrew **baruch atah,** meaning we praise you, the opening of most Hebrew blessings, including **kiddush**, the prayer over wine intoned on Shabbat and other holidays. *Toke* is slang for taking a drag on a marijuana cigarette (aka, a joint).

farklobbered

adj. **Getting so high on weed that distressing thoughts take over and take their toll. Like guilty thoughts about that time you teased your little sister about having *farshtunkener* (stinky) armpits.**

"I was so **farklobbered** last night, my entire life flashed before my eyes. Except later I realized it had been somebody else's life."

Don't tell the true-believer **mushuga-nugs**, but not all weed-induced thoughts and feelings are transcendent insights. Apparently, so I hear, weed smokers sometimes contract a touch of paranoia.

From the Yiddish **farklempt**, meaning choked up with emotion, often despair and guilt, a typically Jewish combination. **Klempt** means clamped, as in having your heart in a vise.

cannabissel

n. **A small amount of pot intake that provides a maintenance high—just enough to take the edge off, but not so much that your grandmother would notice if you visited her afterward.**

"I had a **cannabissel** before I went to my **bubbe's** (grandmother's) the other day. She said I seemed particularly **freylekh** (cheerful)."

And speaking of **bubbe**, it is she who always says, "**Alts in madereyshan**" (everything in moderation).

From the botanical term for marijuana, *cannabis*, and the Yiddish term for little or a small amount, **bissel**.

fonferflowerer

n. **A person who gets so high that they speak in total gibberish.**

"Noah started getting super high before the open-mic poetry nights. He thinks he's a genius but he's a real **fonferflowerer**."

Fonferflowerers are often best understood by those who are equally high or enjoy nonlinear narratives.

From the Yiddish **fonferer**, meaning double-talker, and from *flowerer* (a plant that flowers), mostly because together they form a fun tongue-twister that's close to gibberish itself. (Fun fact: The word *gibberish* sounds like Yiddish, but isn't.)

FREGN NISHT

As any linguist will tell you, expressions change their meanings as the times change, often morphing into opposite meanings. For instance, in English, *awful* used to mean awe-inspiring.

For Yiddish to keep up with the times, it has to spot these transformations. Take the Yiddish expression **fregn nisht**, literally meaning don't ask, and metaphorically meaning there is so much to tell, I can't even begin. But in today's world, the expression now carries an overtone of disapproval, as in, "Don't ask, you aren't really interested anyhow, are you?"

Then there is **chutzpah**, once a clearly derogatory term meaning shameless audacity. These days, in a time seemingly without shame, shameless audacity has become a virtue of sorts, so today one hears, "We need a candidate with formidable **chutzpah** to lead our noble cause."

And then there's our favorite, **meshugana**, which, for as long as we can remember, meant a nutcase or, as **bubbe** used to say, a real "coo-coo fritz." But looking at today's dating sites, we see that **meshuganas** are in demand because they are colorful, humorous, and original, rather than the same-old, same-old types you can find anywhere.

ganjachazer

n. **A pothead who spends so much time in fantasyland that they neglect life in the real world, like washing dishes, sweeping floors, and bathing.**

"I went over to visit that **ganjachazer** Peter and practically needed a snow shovel to make my way from his front door to the couch. What a mess!"

From the Hindi *ganja*, meaning marijuana, and from the Yiddish **chazer**, yet another word for pig and piggish people.

pot shticker

n. **A person who does comedy routines while high, which may or may not be as funny to those unequally medicated.**

"Did you see Selma's **pot shticker** imitation of Nicki Minaj rapping the Gettysburg Address? Sooo funny. Not!"

Shtick is Yiddish for gimmick or comedy routine; *pot* is one of the many terms for marijuana.

cannabidolach

n. **CBD-infused *matzo* balls.**

"After eating a bowl of chicken soup with **Cannabidolach**, even last week's pastrami tastes good."

CBD gives matzo balls a distinctive earthy flavor. If you don't think we need this new, polysyllabic tongue-twister in modern Yiddish, check out your local deli. **Cannabidolach** in chicken soup is hot. Deli people know what's happening out there, baby.

From the Yiddish **kneidlach**, meaning matzo balls, and cannabidiol.

Sederday madness

n. **The celebration of international high holiday Weed Day (April 20, or 4/20) when it coincides with the Seder (the ritual meal on the first night of Passover).**

"Instead of parsley, Mom is putting some kind bud on the Seder plate. It's all in the spirit of **Sederday madness**."

From the Yiddish/Hebrew **Seder**, meaning order, or order of the ritual service, and a riff on the classic alarmist anti-marijuana movie *Reefer Madness*.

blintz krieg

n. **The perpetual production of blintzes, meal after meal, because the cook, usually someone's Polish grandmother, thinks they make for an excellent low-cost dish.**

"I skipped lunch because we're having dinner at Bubbe's, where every day it's a **blintz krieg**."

From the Yiddish **blintz**, a traditional stuffed pancake, and the German *blitzkrieg*, which literally translates to lightning war. **Blintz** came to Yiddish via the Russian *blinets*, meaning little pancake. A **blintz** should not be confused with a blini, which is made with kasha (buckwheat flour). The French think of blintzes as crass crepes.

moogoojew

n. **A Jewish person who regularly eats Chinese food, not only on Christmas. Happily, this old European Jewish tradition lives on at the Wok Garden near you.**

"Zadie has his own booth at Chengdu Taste. He's an **echt** (true) **moogoojew**."

The affinity of Jews for Chinese food has a long and varied history, including the aspect that during the period when Jews were not allowed in German restaurants, Chinese restaurant owners welcomed Jewish clientele. Add to that the fact that Chinese food is dairy-free, a major consideration for those who eat kosher. It has become an entertaining tradition for many Jews to eat at Chinese restaurants on Christmas Eve and Christmas Day. Hey, all the good booths are available.

From the Mandarin *moo goo* (mushrooms).

Briebrei

n. **Matzo brei with melted Brie cheese.**

"Nathan made his **goyishe** wife **Briebrei** for breakfast. She **kvelled** (was delighted)."

So much tastier than **Bubbe's** (Grandmother's) **matzo brei**.

Basically, **matzo brei** is Jewish French toast—bread soaked in egg and fried—except that the bread is unleavened. To me, it has the texture of cardboard left out in the rain, and a similar taste. Maple syrup topping doesn't begin to help. Today's **Jewfoodies** add delicacies to the mix, like French Brie, a soft and subtly mild cheese with a gooey texture to die for.

gnoshaholic

n. **A person who can't stop nibbling on food for virtually the entire day.**

"Razzie is an inveterate **gnoshaholic**. That's why he wears sweatpants with an elastic waistband."

Gnoshaholics tend to make a big show of eating very little at dinner, as if they are on a healthy diet; they also tend to get a bit **zoftig** (plump).

From the Yiddish **gnosh** (or **nosh**,) meaning nibble. Note that fitness types swear that eating multiple very small meals throughout the day is better for one's health than the standard three big meals a day. It is unclear whether eating cupcakes, pizza slices, French fries, and candy bars for these **gnoshes** has improved anyone's health.

fressaholic

n. **A near synonym for *gnoshaholic*, but the actual process of eating is done with animal abandon. Not a pretty sight.**

"Mookie is a **fressaholic**. When he hits the all-you-can-eat buffet, you'll really see the food start to fly."

From the Yiddish **fress**, meaning gluttonous **gnoshing**.

fauxglatt

n. **Kosher fake meat, like the Beyond or Impossible burger, which are kosher because they are made from plants, not animals. The question of whether or not one can eat *fauxglatt* with dairy has yet to be determined, but to be on the safe side, order it with soy cheese.**

"I'm not even kosher, but I still feel virtuous about eating **fauxglatt** burgers."

From the Yiddish word **glatt**, a type of kosher meat in which the lungs of the animal are smooth, without any of the adhesions that would make it **traif** (unkosher).

blitzfress

n. **Eating in excess when high on marijuana, aka experiencing a case of the munchies.**

"I went on a mad **blitzfress** and ate an entire extra-large Memphis BBQ chicken pizza."

This is why marijuana is sometimes recommended to people on weight-gaining diets.

From *blitzed*, slang for stoned, and the Yiddish **fress**, meaning to gobble nonstop.

schmearfusion

n. **A spread (usually cream cheese) that has other food items mixed into it, like bits of lox, lemon zest, poppy seeds, dried cranberries, walnuts, capers or—God forbid—bacon.**

"Have you heard about this crazy new **schmearfusion**, dark chocolate in hummus? I might give that one a pass."

Schmear is a Yiddish verb meaning to spread onto, or a noun meaning that thing that is spread, as in a **shmear** of cream cheese. The vehicle for the **schmear** is usually a bagel. **Schmear** has become so common that it has entered American slang. Who doesn't like a good **schmear**?

patshke disorder

n. **A neurotic condition of culinarians who endlessly mess around in the kitchen without ever getting the meal on the table.**

"Ever since he got that fancy new Cuisinart, David has developed **patshke disorder**."

This comes from the Yiddish word **patshken**, to daub or schmear, which has become generalized to mean to mess around, dawdle, or engage in a random, unproductive activity in any room in the house, not just the kitchen.

milchigas

n. **The gas generated in the *kishkas* (intestines) by people afflicted with lactose intolerance, often unpleasant for the people around the afflicted one.**

"It's **farshtunken** (stinky) in here. **Milchigas**! Who put cream in **Zayde's** (Grandpa's) coffee?"

Milchig is Yiddish for dairy and dairy products. In kosher cooking, **milchig** cannot be combined with **fleishig** (meat). *Gas* refers to flatulence.

challahday

n. **Cute slang for the Sabbath, during which challah (braided egg bread) is traditionally baked and eaten. The term has been generalized to mean any special day or vacation day, with or without bread.**

"Morris and I had such a lovely **challahday**, I could **plotz** (collapse)."

The word **challah** has a long and appropriately twisted history, and similar braided egg breads can be found in Belarus, Ukraine, Russia, and even South Africa. French toast made with **challah** and topped with cinnamon is served in high-tone brunch restaurants.

meshugluten

n. **A person who is irrationally convinced they have celiac disease and therefore cannot tolerate any wheat products.**

"Until Abe's doctor found that he had an ulcer, Abe was another crazy **meshugluten**."

Meshuglutens are everywhere these days. **Meshuglutenitis** has replaced restless leg syndrome as the hypochondriasis du jour.

From the Yiddish **meshugana**, meaning a crazy person.

présentation panik bafaln

n. **The panic attack experienced by hosts of dinner parties over the aesthetic appearance of the food on serving plates.**

"Yes, there are only six string beans on each plate, but I've arranged them to look like six-pointed stars. No **présentation panik bafaln** for me."

Now that *la présentation* of food has superseded the importance of food's quantity (or taste, for that matter), hosts worry about it the way they used to worry about not having enough food for guests. The latter used to be known as Jewish Food Panic (JFP), often resulting in preparing enough food for a battalion in order to serve eight people.

From the Yiddish **panik bafaln**, meaning panic attack.

schmendrink

n. **A ludicrous, super-sweet cocktail. Think a mix of ginger liqueur and raspberry-lime sorbet.**

"That's Carl's fifth **schmendrink** of the night. Boy, he's going to feel that in the morning."

The days of going bottoms-up on a jigger of whiskey are giving way to the age of complicated, mixological **schmendrinks**, when even getting smashed leaves a sweet aftertaste.

From the Yiddish **schmendrick**, meaning a fool.

balegula's balagula

n. **Junk food pastries, often stuffed full of sweet goo, favored by sweet-toothed youngsters and *meshuga-nugs*. A treat without pretension.**

"Morty doesn't go anywhere without his bag of **balegula's balagula**."

From the Yiddish **balegula**, meaning a person of low standing, and from the Italian balagula, meaning a thin-crusted, flaky, and delicate pastry.

5

INSULTS AND COMPLAINTS

neo-shanda

n. **Insults for today's world.**

"It's become hard for me to know when Greta is insulting me because I'm not up to date on her **neo-shanda** taunts."

In traditional Yiddish, the number of words for various complaints is only rivaled by the number of insult words. But following the principle that the more you've got, the more you've got to complain about, new insult words are sorely needed. You're welcome!

From the Yiddish **shanda**, meaning shame or disgrace.

hipkvetch

n. **Complaints about things so obscure you've probably never heard of them.**

"Sonja always has these **hipkvetches** about her new favorite band being discovered by hipsters, so she now has to find another one. Why even bother? It's either that or the bodega's run out of her favorite artisanal pickles again."

There's always something new to complain about.

From the Yiddish **kvetch**, meaning to complain.

polischmerz

n. **The quality of having a dismal or depressing view of the national or world political situation. Which just about everybody has these days.**

"Rachel has such a case of **polischmerz**; she just sits and watches videos of cartoon bears all day on her phone."

From the Yiddish word **schmerz**, meaning pain, which comes directly from a German word of the same meaning, as in *weltschmerz*, a generalized feeling of melancholy and world-weariness.

appschvitz

n. **The result of being annoyed or made anxious by one's inability to get one's smartphone to work as desired, particularly as quickly as desired. More generally, it can cover any computer- or phone-based frustration.**

"It took me literally more than a minute to get ahold of Saul. Like I have all the time in the world. Such **appschvitz** I felt."

This new anxiety raises the question of whether our lives have become more efficient via electronic aids or just more fragmented.

From the Yiddish word **schvitz**, meaning to sweat, or metaphorically, to be nervous or anxious.

CURSES

FOR MODERN TIMES

"May your health insurance provider decide that constipation is a preexisting condition!"

Long Yiddish curses are renowned for their elaborate plot twists. This one is an update of **Oyf doktoyrim zol er dos avekgebn** (He should give it all away to doctors).

"May you sell everything and retire to Florida just as global warming makes it uninhabitable!"

This one is a variation of many old Yiddish curses; for example, "A hundred houses shall he have, in every house a hundred rooms and in every room twenty beds, and a delirious fever should drive him from bed to bed."

"May you be convinced that you have gluten intolerance, lyme disease, and restless leg syndrome, even though all your tests come back negative!"

This one is reminiscent of the fabulous old Yiddish curse, "May your tapeworm develop constipation while trolley cars run through your intestine as thieves camp out in your belly and steal your guts one by one."

"You should emerge from the desert scorched and parched to find before you a luxury hotel with one thousand empty rooms, but they don't accept AmEx extra points!"

For unknown reasons, Yiddish curses are obsessed with multi-roomed hotels that turn out to be bad news. One old-time favorite is "You should own a hotel with one thousand rooms and have a bellyache in each one!"

"He should invest all his mother's money in a start-up that no one understands and evaporates her money."

In the old days, Yiddish curses often involved ill wishes for the cursed one's businesses and stores. As in, "He should have a large store, and whatever people ask for he shouldn't have, and what he does have shouldn't be requested."

"May all the awful things your ex says about you mysteriously appear on your LinkedIn page!"

This one is loosely inspired by the classic "All problems I have in my heart should go to his head."

"After walking twelve blocks with your thighs squeezed together in a desperate search for a public restroom, may you find one at a fancy restaurant, but be barred from entering because you aren't wearing a tie!"

A riff on the old "May you fall into the outhouse just as a regiment of soldiers is finishing a prune stew and twelve barrels of beer."

loch in kop of kindness

n. **An empty gesture of kindness.**

"Selma says, 'I worry about you constantly,' but she can't even look up from her phone while she's saying it. It's about as heartfelt as any **loch in kop of kindness**."

From the Yiddish expression **loch in kop**, literally meaning a hole in the head, commonly used ironically in the phrase **Ich darf es vi a loch in kop** (I need this like I need a hole in the head).

grepse for thanks

n. **A blatant absence of appreciation for, or a rude and callow response to, a favor or gift.**

"After Mischa drove Ben to the train station, no 'thank you.' Not even a friendly nod. Just a **grepse for thanks**."

From the Yiddish **grepse**, meaning burp. This expression is adapted from the Dutch *stank voor dank* (a stink for a thank you). **Grepse** sounds like a **grepse**, starting way back in the throat, where all Yiddish begins.

fake-kaktah

adj. **Pretending to be a wild, colorfully kooky person but not fooling anyone.**

"There Millie goes with that **fake-kaktah** laugh again."

In these days of internet-famous personalities, self-promotion, and influencer creep, **fake-kaktah** abounds.

From the Yiddish **fakakta**, meaning ridiculous, especially in behavior. The original meaning was fouled up, with the emphasis on *foul*—**kakta** literally means doo-doo. How a word for excrement morphed into meaning "ridiculously silly" is only understood by linguists under the age of five.

toxipupik

n. **A person who possesses a toxic personality down to their very core. Everyone who encounters them feels *shreklekh* (awful) afterward.**

"Every time she has to negotiate a deal, Franny brings Max with her. He is such a **toxipupik** that buyers will sign anything just to get away from him."

Combining the sadly common modern concept of the toxic personality and the old Yiddish **pupik**, meaning navel. In Yiddish culture, the belly button is the seat of the soul, the basic person, the place from which we all began.

blankenshpiel

n. **A political speech or statement that is so vague it neither offends nor informs anyone.**

"Her stump speech manages to be both for and against raising taxes on the middle class. It's a regular **blankenshpiel.**"

From the Yiddish **shpiel**, meaning a sales pitch.

TSUMISHT SLANG

American slang has always been a melting pot of languages—a French word here, a Spanish phrase there, a dollop of Russian, a pinch of Yiddish. It makes for a tasty **tzimmes** (stew).

The high point, of course, is when slang words of different linguistic origins get **tsumisht** (mixed) in a single phrase. Like when an American tourist we know was visiting a shul in Havana, Cuba, he was warned by the tour guide to beware the **schnoristas.** (**Schnorrer** is Yiddish for a beggar, and *-ista* is a Spanish suffix that denotes someone associated with something and appears frequently in American slang, as in *fashionista*.)

Another favorite was heard in New York's Little Italy. Two men were arguing and one shouted, "*Baciami* my **tush**!" which combines the Italian imperative for *kiss* with the Yiddish for, well, **tush**. That is to say, "Kiss my ass," an international expression of contempt of unknown etymology. Like many combos, "*Baciami* my **tush**" has a lovely rhythm, all of its own.

And this one had an entire café laughing: A young Jewish man appeared at the door with a gorgeous, blue-eyed blonde on his arm, and a friend cheered, "*Viva la* **shikses** (non-Jewish women)!"

Indeed, *viva la* linguistic **tzimmes**!

swollen prostak

n. **The quality of a vulgar, ignorant person who believes themselves to be classy and clever.**

"Turn off your hearing aids, here comes Eddie and his **swollen prostak**."

From the Yiddish **prostak**, meaning an ignorant boor.

heymishcamer

n. **Someone who tries to pass himself off as just a regular guy but is actually something quite different; a scammer.**

"Beware Gary Westheimer. With a smile and a pat on the shoulders, he'll glad-hand you out of your life's savings. A real **heymischcamer**."

From the Yiddish **heymish**, meaning homey or quaint.

schmutzlinguist

n. **Someone who is adept at inventing caustic and damning expressions about others.**

"This Danny Klein character packed his book *Schmegoogle* with lots of colorful insults. A real **schmutzlinguist** he is."

From the Yiddish **schmutz**, meaning dirt.

alter kvetcher/alter kicker

n. **An old fart who either complains about their age (*alter kvetcher*) or thinks they have the energy of someone half their age (*alter kicker*), as in "still kicking after all these years."**

"I can do more push-ups than my video game addict son. I'm a genuine **alter kicker**."

Reminiscent of the story about Mel Goldfarb, eighty-two, who got a personal trainer and groomer who made him look twenty years younger. Then Mel got run over by a bus. When he asked God why him, why now, God said, "To tell you the truth, Goldfarb, I didn't recognize you."

Alter kicker is derived from the Yiddish term **alter kocker**, which literally means old shitter.

alter kockamamie

n. **The nonsequential, somewhat nonsensical conversations of senior citizens with faulty hearing and short-term memory loss.**

"I went over there for the gin rummy game and it was pure **alter kockamamie** from her: 'What's his name, you know, the one whose daughter . . . maybe not. Somebody's daughter. Every woman is, you know. Whew, somebody needs a shower. Or is that the soup?'"

From **alter kocker**, Yiddish for old fart, and *cockamamie*, which sounds like it could be Yiddish but is not.

schmatta-chic

adj. **The quality of person who wears worn or old clothes as a fashion statement.**

"There goes Hilda in her ripped jeans looking oh-so-voguish. I hear she buys them new and then has her maid rip them with pinking shears. **Schmatta-chic**!"

This compound term is derived from *shabby-chic*, meaning the intentionally decorative appearance of being worn down, such as painted furniture with the wood grain showing or faded jeans with the knees worn through. And **schmatta** is Yiddish for rag, which has come to mean dress, as in, "Ralph Lauren (né Ralph Lifshitz) is in the **schmatta** business." It can also mean an old or unstylish piece of clothing. **Schmatta-chic** is another mild put-down, leavened with a **bissel** (little) admiration.

kvellkill

v. **To brag so much and so often, particularly about one's children, as to completely bore the listener.**

"And she said to me, 'Did I tell you that Joshie got into the best kindergarten in Manhattan?' **Kvellkill**!"

Derived from the Yiddish **kvell**, meaning to experience pride in someone else, typically one's children. The very appearance of the term **kvellkill** raises the question of whether or not today's Jewish parents **kvell** about their children more than other parents do. Huh? Is the Pope a **goy** (gentile)? This new Yiddish insult is usually only uttered in a whisper.

ballebuster

n. **Someone who makes men feel emasculated.**

"Morty wakes up to his husband **geschreiing** (yelling) that he sleeps like a **chazzer** (pig). What a way to start your day. Such a **ballebuster**!"

Directly from the Yiddish word **balebosteh**, meaning an expert homemaker, a woman who has everything totally under control. Some etymologists believe that **balebosteh** is related to the word *alabaster* because a **balebosteh** knows from keeping the alabaster clean and shiny.

WASP tam

n. **Emulating the taste of a WASP, as in wearing a silk paisley foulard around your neck.**

"First he changed his name from Mordecai Sanberg to Pierce Simmons, and then it was the double-breasted blazers, Oxford shirts, tie pins, the whole **megillah** (Yiddish/Hebrew for "the entire scroll," but figuratively "the whole nine yards.") **WASP tam** on parade!"

From WASP, white Anglo-Saxon Protestant, and the Yiddish **tam**, meaning taste. To suggest that a Jew has **WASP tam** can either be an opprobrium or a compliment. It's a point-of-view thing.

mayn eltere shvester's tam

n. **To have out-of-date and tacky taste; literally, to have my older sister's taste.**

"Mindy is so day-before-yesterday. Look at that haircut! **Mayn eltere shvester's tam**. *Passé plus*!"

From the Yiddish insult **mayn bobes ta**, literally meaning "my grand-mother's taste," also meaning out-of-date and tacky, but because tastes now change from one meme to the next, this expression had to be brought up to date.

schlockbroker

n. **Someone who sells worthless items, especially stocks and stock options.**

"Ten people I know got ripped off by that **schlockbroker** Bernie Madoff. Such a **shanda** (shame or scandal)!"

From the Yiddish **schlock**, meaning cheap or shoddy.

schmatta pants

n. **A person who thinks they are very smart but aren't.**

"Oy, there goes Mickey again, pontificating on Marxism. So he got a PhD in economics; he's still a **phudnik** (over-educated bore). Mickey has lox for brains. He's a **schmatta pants**."

This word makes little sense and came into use simply because it's a pun, and a bad one at that. **Schmatta** sounds wee bit like *smart*. But **schmatta** actually means rag, which evolved into meaning an article of clothing. Someone in the **schmatta** business manufactures clothing. Adding to this term's ridiculousness is the fact that **schmatta pants** actually does mean something: to wit, an article of clothing called pants.

AI-seykhl

n. **Literally meaning to have the intelligence of a computer program, but the term is used sarcastically to imply a person lacks common sense, imagination, and compassion.**

"You think Herschel is smart? To me, all he's got is **AI-seykhl**."

AI is the abbreviation for artificial intelligence, a computer system that is able to perform tasks that normally require human intelligence. And from the Yiddish **seykhl**, meaning intelligence that is informed by common sense.

lign in drerd un bakn éclairs

phr. **An updated version of the old Yiddish curse *Lign in drerd un bakn beygl!* (Lie in the dirt and bake bagels!), with the added implication of "You think you're so fancy with your French baking."**

"You stole my cheesecake recipe and passed it off as your own. What kind of friend does such a thing? May you **lign in drerd un bakn éclairs**!"

Where the original curse came from is unknown—perhaps spontaneously out of the mouth of an angry housewife in Lithuania. Spontaneous **shtetl** (small town) poetry.

feh! fetishist

n. **People who are incessantly on the lookout for something that will disgust them, say a speck of *schmutz* (dirt) on their collar.**

"Maxine can't stop picking at her daughter's sweater. She finds dirt everywhere. And if she can't find it, I think she puts it there. A regular **Feh! fetishist**."

From the Yiddish exclamation **Feh!**, an expression of disgust.

kibbitzoporific

adj. **The tendency to induce sleep with one's endless, mindless chatter.**

"You know what's better than Ambien? Sitting down with Barney when he's in a particularly loquacious mood. The man is downright **kibbitzoporific**."

From the Yiddish **kibbitz**, meaning the act of interminable annoying yakking, and *soporific*, meaning sedative.

slapshtick

n. **Old-fashioned and long-winded humor. For example, the endless, detailed, and nuanced jokes told at Catskill resorts in the mid-twentieth century.**

"Uncle Morty is doing his after-dinner **slapshtick** again. It's kinda fun, if you have a spare hour or two."

From the Yiddish **shtick**, meaning comic routine, and slapstick, meaning broad physical comedy, like throwing a pie in someone's face for a laugh.

schmortification

n. **The humiliation experienced by a fool who has the sudden realization of just how foolish they appear to others; an epiphany of sorts.**

"After Uncle Morty finally came to the end of his hour-long joke, nobody laughed. Or even smiled. You could see him blanche with **schmortification**. Poor Uncle Morty."

From the Yiddish **schmo**, metaphorically meaning a jerk or a fool, but literally meaning a penis. The two meanings appear to be intertwined, so to speak.

6

HEALTH AND ANXIETY

tchotchkompulsive

n. **A behavior disorder in which the afflicted person cannot resist buying any *tchotchke* that presents itself. Say, that one-inch-tall plastic mule on the dollar table at the neighbor's garage sale, or the tin sheriff's star at that "Save the Trees" fundraiser, or the cracked porcelain mug emblazoned with the words *I've had better* at the temple charity drive.**

"Phyllis is such a **tchotchkompulsive** that she had to put an addition onto her house just to accommodate her collection. God forbid she should throw out a single one."

In **tchotchkompulsiveness**, the possessions hoarded are restricted to small, sickeningly cute, worthless, and particularly prone-to-being-tripped-over objects.

Tchotchke is old Yiddish (via Slavic) for small, sickeningly cute, worthless, stumbled-over objects. One wry lexicographer defines **tchotchkes** as "the stuff left behind after your house has been burgled."

helio hocker

n. **A parent who is obsessed with their child's school grades, popularity, and mental and physical health.**

"Elizabeth is sending her five-year-old to a shrink because she thinks he is underperforming in kindergarten—something about his clumsiness at cutting along a line with scissors. A regular **helio hocker**, Elizabeth is."

Helio (Greek in origin) is an adaptation of *helicopter*, referring to the now all-too-common term *helicopter parenting*: the practice of monitoring every moment of one's child's life, then immediately correcting any faults discovered. In old Yiddish, **hock** and **hocker** meant to bang. The phrase **hock my chinik** (bang my teakettle), is a metaphor for seriously getting on my nerves, or giving me a headache.

IT'S DUTCH TO ME

Leaving a shoe store in Amsterdam, a tourist from New York heard the shopkeeper call after him, "**Mazel!**"

Mazel, of course, is Yiddish, and is usually coupled with **tov** to mean, roughly, "Good luck." (**Mazel**'s roots are in Jewish mysticism, where it describes the roots of the soul.)

Later, the tourist asked a Dutch friend why the shopkeeper had spoken to him in Yiddish.

"That's just regular Amsterdam slang," the friend said. "He had no idea it was a Yiddish word." Before the War, Amsterdam was a quarter Jewish, and lots of Yiddish words slipped into the language. After the war, most of the Jews were gone, but the slang remained.

So today Amsterdam slang is chock-full of Yiddish words like **afgepeigerd** (a corpse), **smoesje** (a white lie), **ponum** (a face), and hundreds more.

The affinity of the Dutch for Yiddish may, in part, have a phonetic origin: The Dutch word part *sch* is pronounced similarly to the Yiddish *sch*. In both languages, the *ch* erupts from so deep in the throat that it is mistaken by foreigners as the result of postnasal drip.

With any luck, our friends in the Netherlands will find new riches to expand their slang lexicon in this book.

tsuriasis

n. **A psychogenic skin disorder; literally, a worry wart.**

"Sandy says she has poison ivy but, with all her fighting with her mother, I bet it's **tsuriasis**."

From the old Yiddish **tsuris**, meaning troubles, and the emotional state these troubles put a person in. And from the English *psoriasis*, meaning a skin disease that produces red, itchy patches.

krank crank

n. **A person who is forever complaining about their health even if they seem to be perfectly well. A noisy hypochondriac.**

"Milton was whining about his teeth all day. Yesterday it was his hemorrhoids. Such a **krank crank** he is, I'm telling you, I can't tell you."

From the Yiddish **krank**, meaning sickness.

farshlepteh cranky

adj. **The state of a person who is always in a bad mood, even when good things happen. The attitude of a perennial *kvetcher* (complainer).**

"Don't even bother telling a joke to Mitzi. She won't laugh. She's **farshlepteh cranky**."

From the old Yiddish **farshlepteh krenk**, meaning endlessly sick, but often generalized to mean anything endless, like a **farshlepteh krenk** sermon.

gesuntnik

n. **A person who is forever boasting about their good health and fitness, particularly a senior citizen. The opposite of a *krank crank*.**

"Here comes Sophie in her jogging togs again. Yesterday it was her biking **schmatta**. Such a **gesuntnik** she is, I'm telling you, I can't tell you."

From the Yiddish **gesunt**, meaning good health.

gesuntaholic

n. **Someone who is obsessed with the state of their health 24/7.**

"So today Simon is seeing Dr. Patel for a *third* opinion about his hemorrhoids. He's a regular **gesuntaholic**."

Also from the Yiddish **gesunt**, meaning good health.

psych 101–nik

n. **A person who is forever psychologically analyzing other people's motives and behavior. *Pscyh 101–nikking* is an increasingly popular subject of conversation, a kind of educated gossip.**

"There goes Ruthy, the **psych 101–nik** again. She claims that what Izzy really meant when he said, 'Pass the salt, Mom,' was 'You ruined my life, Mother.'"

The suffix **-nik** is Yiddish derived from Russian and refers to people who support or are associated with a particular political cause or cultural attitude (e.g. beatnik, no-goodnik, peacenik, etc.). *Psych 101* refers to the basic psychology course taught in most liberal arts colleges.

oy-yoy-yoy-yoyo

n. **A labile person; one given to rapid, repetitive mood swings.**

"Poor Edith, her moods change faster than her daughter changes boyfriends. Edith is certifiable **oy-yoy-yoy-yoyo**."

From the Yiddish **oy-yoy-yoy**, a vocalization of grief.

gifilted

adj. **Stuffed or filled up with anything—originally with food but now also with, say, too much work or a strong emotion.**

"I'm **gifilted** with grief."

From the Yiddish **gefilte fish**, meaning stuffed fish. Like many foods, **gefilte fish** has smoothly passed from culture to culture without so much as a **grepse** (burp). The Polish term for gefilte fish is translated as carp Jewish-style and is often served on Christmas Eve and Holy Saturday.

schvitz yoga

n. **The practice of yoga exercises inside a hot and humid enclosure, a new trend.**

"After hearing about this new business of **schvitz yoga**, old-time-**schvitzer** Mordecai said, 'What's all this bending and twisting about? In the **schvitz**, one sits and talks. That's it.'"

Historical note: In the old days, a requirement for the job of throwing buckets of water on the **shvitzers** was that the attendant be deaf and thus unable to hear the gossip and business deals being discussed therein.

From the Yiddish **shvitz**, to sweat. Also used as a noun: the **shvitz**, the place where one takes a sweat bath, an old practice for Eastern European Jews.

tsu sakh disorder

n. **Anxiety caused by too-muchness, whether it is too much stuff in the house, too many responsibilities, or too many people coming for dinner.**

"Rachel says she is beside herself with **tsu sakh disorder**, but her husband says that's impossible because the house is so full of **tchotchkes** (small collectible objects) that there's no room beside herself."

From the Yiddish **tsu sakh**, meaning too much.

shpilkes pills

n. **Prescription medication to calm a person down.**

"Melvin keeps switching his **shpilkes pills**. So far he's tried Xanax, Klonopin, and Lorazepam in hopes of finally quelling his anxiety."

From the Yiddish **shpilkes**, meaning excessive nervous energy, often manifested in physical tics, such as bouncing one's legs up and down while sitting.

farmisht muscles

n. **Muscles that are confused and shocked by new exercise routines. According to exercise gurus and body-builders, this is a good thing. Shocked and confused muscles build mass faster.**

"Tante Tania says, 'Better **farmisht muscles** than **farmisht** in the **kop** (head).'"

From the Yiddish **farmisht**, literally meaning twisted out of shape, but generally used to mean confused.

farklempt disorder

n. **A personality disorder in which people cannot express their feelings because of excess emotion.**

"Arnold loves Sol so much, but because of his **farklempt disorder**, he can't tell him so."

Were Freud alive today, he would include a whole chapter on **farklempt disorder** in his seminal work, *The Psychopathology of Everyday Life*.

From the Yiddish **farklempt**, literally meaning choked up. Note that **farklempt disorder** is sometimes equated with passive-aggressive behavior, in which people express their negative feelings subtly through their actions instead of handling them directly. Others consider this kind of behavior politeness.

hotzeplotz phase

n. **A period of life when a person feels lost and aimless, often experienced by young people just out of college.**

"Ever since Myron got his PhD in philosophy, he doesn't know what to do with himself except debate the meaning of life. We hope it's just his **hotzeplotz phase**."

From the Yiddish **hotzeplotz**, meaning the middle of nowhere.

boomerang broygus

n. **The sullen, unmotivated, distracted state of mind experienced by young college graduates who have returned to live with their parents, usually for financial reasons.**

"Myron just mopes around the house, occasionally mumbling to his parents, 'Maybe you should throw me out, but where would I go?' Sounds like the first stage of **boomerang broygus**."

From the Yiddish **broygus**, meaning, sullen, morose, and quiet. And from the contemporary American expression *boomerang kids*, meaning young adults who return to live with their parents before taking off on their own again. This pattern has been known to repeat like, well, a boomerang.

tsurits syndrome

n. **A tic disorder in which individuals uncontrollably shout out whatever is troubling them at any given moment.**

"Rodney shouts '**oy**' about everything, like even when his nose itches. He's got **tsurits syndrome**."

From the Yiddish **tsuris**, meaning worry and suffering, and Tourette's syndrome, a disorder characterized by involuntary, repetitive movements and vocalizations.

umglick shammer

n. **A person who pretends to have bad luck in order to elicit pity and win favors.**

"What an **umglick shammer** that Milton is. He's told me three times now that his **bubbe** (grandmother) passed away, when we all know she's the picture of health in Boca Raton."

From the Yiddish **umglick**, meaning an unlucky person.

vey-is-mir-nik

n. **A person who is forever dramatizing the suffering they endure or believe they endure.**

"That **vey-is-mir-nik** Asher gets on my nerves. Today he was **oy**ing about how his hair is falling out from too much worry."

From the Yiddish **vey is mir**, meaning I am pain itself. **Vey is mir** is often preceded by **oy**.

binge blechedich

adj. **The pallid, sickly state of a person who has been bingeing on a television series for innumerable hours.**

"After watching twelve straight hours of *Downton Abbey*, Charlotte grew faint and couldn't stand up. The ER doctor diagnosed it as **binge blechedich**."

From the Yiddish **blechedich**, meaning lifeless and sickly.

schmalingerer

n. **A person who not only feigns illness or injury in order to avoid work, but does so in a totally ridiculous and unbelievable way.**

"Frank left the store early because he said he suffered from intense pain. 'Where's the pain?' his father asked, and Frank replied, 'Everywhere. It keeps traveling around my body.' Sounds like a **schmalingerer** to me."

From the Yiddish **schmaltz**, literally meaning animal fat, but metaphorically meaning tacky behavior and taste. And from the English *malingerer*, meaning to fake an illness, especially in order to shirk one's duty.

7 PEOPLE YOU MEET

kiboshibboleth

n. **A personal agenda to put an end to all existing government programs; libertarianism.**

"Sophie is such a **kiboshibboleth**, she'd turn away the fire department if her house was on fire."

From the Yiddish **kibosh**, meaning to squelch, and the English-via-Hebrew **shibboleth**, meaning a saying or maxim used by adherents of a particular principle.

schmeglitchnik

n. **A person given to constantly making small mistakes, especially when delivering a speech.**

"Mordecai has to start the same sentence over fifteen times before he gets it right. And half the time, he still doesn't get it right. That's the way it goes when you're a **schmeglitchnik**."

From the Yiddish prefix **sch-**, most often used in put-down words like **schmendrick** and **schlimazel**. And from the English *glitch,* meaning a minor malfunction. *Glitch* may itself have Yiddish roots, derived from the word **glitsh**, meaning slippery place.

ganifocrat

n. **A politician who is a thief or conman. Hard to imagine, but apparently such people exist.**

"The personal library of the chair of the library trustees has expanded incredibly. Methinks she's a **ganifocrat**."

From the Yiddish **ganif**, meaning a thief or crook.

schmegridster

n. **A committee member given to slowing all proposals to a halt.**

"Ever since Vicky joined the historic building commission, nothing gets done. What a **schmegridster**! Last week, she insisted on doing a PowerPoint presentation on different kinds of bricks before they could take a vote on repairing a wall."

Also from the Yiddish prefix **schme-**, and from the English *gridlock*, meaning the obstruction of progress by partisan rancor.

tzimmesocrat

n. **A committee member who inflates the importance of minor initiatives.**

"Ever since Janice joined the Clean Streets Board, the streets have gotten dirtier because of those **fakaktah** (ridulous) cat litter boxes she puts on every corner. Another tedious **tzimmesocrat**!"

From the Yiddish **tzimmes**, meaning a stew of sweetened veggies and fruit. It evolved to mean to make a big fuss over something small, because **tzimmes** cooks traditionally complain about the slicing and dicing involved in its preparation.

piddle kemfer

n. **A person who devotes himself to minor, often ridiculous, causes.**

"Max is gathering signatures for his homeless guinea pig initiative. He's a regular **piddle kemfer**."

From the Yiddish **kemfer**, meaning fighter.

lantzmanish

n. **A non-Jew who frequently acts and thinks like a Jew by, for example, sprinkling Yiddish in their speech, gesturing animatedly with their hands, and considering every issue from forty-seven different points of view.**

"What is it with that wannabe Pierce Watkins saying he wants to keep kosher? Such a **lantzmanish**."

From the Yiddish **lantzman**, meaning fellow countryman or fellow Jew.

oy-oy-7

n. **An incompetent spy.**

"After Bernie started wearing his CIA sweatshirt to the gym, the Agency finally had to dismiss him. Bernie claimed he was only trying to blend in. This is why they call him **Oy-Oy-7**."

From the Yiddish **oy vey** an expression of exasperation, and from the popular British fictional spy James Bond, whose code name is 007.

THE HILARIOUS SOUNDS OF YIDDISH

Everybody knows that the intonation of Yiddish phrases is smile-inducing—its sing-songy delivery, its unexpected emphasis on the "wrong" syllables, the substitution of *oi* for *r*, as in *hoit* instead of *hurt*. In linguistics, the study of melody, pitch, pause, and intonation is called prosody, and Yiddish is a prosodist's dream language.

But it is not only the intonation of Yiddish phrases that tickles; it is also its phonetics. Mel Brooks famously said that the sound *k* is the funniest in the English language. *Salmon* does not sound funny, he said, but *turkey*? Hilarious!

Brooks, an MOT (Member of the Tribe), undoubtedly had Yiddish in mind, too, with its funny-sounding words like **kibbitz** (to mindlessly gab), which has the added comical toot of a *tz*. Not to mention **kitzel** (to tickle), which does exactly what it promises. And, of course, there are those double *k* whammies, **kishkas** (intestines), which can make one laugh so hard that it hurts down there, and **fakakta**, a word, among many, for what the **kishkas** deliver at their endpoint.

Add to this the fact that intoning Yiddish feels good in the mouth. In his popular book *Alphabet Juice*, American humorist Roy Blount Jr. maintains that some words are connected to their meaning because they are "sonicky"—they are fun to articulate. Like the word *squelch*: You start with that easy *s* sound, push out your lips for the middle part, hit the roof of your mouth with your tongue, and end up with a little explosion.

"As if bursting a grape," Blount says.

What could be more "sonicky" than the Yiddish word **shpilkes** (nervous energy)? The mouth **kvells** (is delighted).

tzaddik-dick

n. **A person who passes himself off as a holy man; the "chosen one."**

"Artie walked up to the Sabrett hot dog stand and said, 'Make me one with everything,' and next thing you know, he's a Buddhist with this own ashram . . . in Brooklyn. He's a genuine **tzaddik-dick**."

From the Yiddish **tzaddik**, a saint or holy man. *Dick* is American slang for a penis or, metaphorically, a jerk.

vitzaddict

n. **A person who compulsively jokes about everything, no matter how serious the subject at hand is.**

"We were talking about cancer and Milton chimes in with a mother-in-law gag. **Vitzaddict**!"

From the Yiddish **vitz**, meaning joke or wisecrack.

klutzcop

n. **An uncommonly clumsy policeman, particularly a traffic cop whose erratic arm waving causes accidents.**

"So this **klutzcop** signals me to turn, ignoring the fact that there's a ten-ton track doing the same thing."

From the Yiddish **klutz**, meaning clumsy, awkward.

farfoilt finder

n. **A person, often an older relative, who delights in rooting out spoiled items in the refrigerator, particularly the refrigerator of someone she is visiting.**

"Oy veh, somebody get Aunt Sonia out of our kitchen or she'll throw out this morning's milk because she thinks it smells funny. She's the family **farfoilt finder**."

From the Yiddish **farfoilt**, meaning spoiled, rotten.

JewBu-nik

n. **A Jew who practices Buddhism, sometimes blending the two traditions, like combining *davening* (rocking forward and back while standing) with Buddhist vipassana meditation. The most famous *JewBu-nik*: the late Leonard Cohen.**

"There goes Lenny, washing the feet of his **bhikkhu** (Buddhist monk) while humming "Hava Nagila." He's the original **JewBu-nik**."

The term **JewBu**, a Jew who practices Buddhism, was first brought into slang via the publication of *The Jew in the Lotus* (1994) by Rodger Kamenetz. The suffix **-nik** is Yiddish derived from Russian and refers to people who support or are associated with a particular political cause or cultural attitude. It's ubiquitous these days: Not just in beatnik, no-goodnik, and peacenik, but in right-to-life-nik, global warming–nik, classical music–nik, and Tin Pan Alley–nik. It's become a reflexive stop word or phrase, like *you know* or *yup*, appended to everything one says. People are becoming *nik*-niks.

phudnik

n. **An irritating bore with a PhD; any overeducated bore.**

"Ever since Barney got his PhD in social psychology, he starts every sentence with the phrase 'Existentially speaking . . .' It is to **genets** (yawn), like with all **phudniks**."

From the Yiddish **nudnik**, meaning a pestering, irritating bore.

nebishottie

n. **A stumbling, ineffectual nobody whose looks are unlovely, yet who still manages to attract sexual partners in a major way.**

"Don't ask me how Morty gets all those beautiful women. He has the face of a **tsherepakhe** (turtle) and the personality of a gefilte fish. Another **nebishottie** mystery of a man."

From the Yiddish **nebish**, meaning someone who is helpless and hapless.

draycup of human kindness

n. **A person who cages drinks at a bar by begging shamelessly, trying to appeal to people's altruism.**

"Oy veh, here comes Viola, with her **draycup of human kindness** melodrama. Hang on to your credit cards."

Draycup is Yiddish for a turned-around head; figuratively, it refers to someone who is perpetually confused and confusing. Also from "the milk of human kindness," which originated in *Macbeth* and means compassion or sympathy.

shlum schlump

n. **A person who is dedicated to making peace among friends and family members yet always ends up making things worse.**

"Sophie wasn't speaking to Iris, so Myron, that **shlum schlump**, entered the scene, and now Sophie isn't speaking to Iris, Meredith, or Myron."

From the Yiddish **shlum**, meaning peace, by way of the Hebrew **shalom**, meaning the same. A **shlum-makher** is a peacemaker. And **schlump** is Yiddish for a person who is inept. Somewhere along the line, the echo phrase, **shlum, shlum** entered American slang, apparently just because it's fun to say and sing.

selfie schlemiel

n. **A person obsessed with taking selfies, usually several every day, which are kept in a folder for viewing, also several times daily.**

"Why Mel is a **selfie schlemiel** is anybody's guess. Maybe it's because he knows his **punim** (face) is instantly forgettable."

From the Yiddish **schlemiel**, a clumsy and inept fool.

botox balegan

n. **A Botox cosmetic procedure run amok, leaving the patient's face a cartoonish mess. Even worse, it's not covered by health insurance.**

"If it hadn't been for the caption, I never would have recognized him. Oy, what a **Botox balegan** he had!"

Any mention here of specific movie star **Botox balegans** have been omitted out of **tsdkh** (charity).

From the Yiddish **balegan**, meaning a total sloppy mishmash; *mishmash*, by the way, is another word that some linguists mistakenly believe to be Yiddish in origin.

ALPHABETICAL LIST OF TERMS

ACKNOWLEDGMENTS

I WISH TO THANK Rachel Shukert and Aaron Spiegel for their original neo-Yiddishisms. Also, Daniel Bialowas and Samara Q. Klein, for cluing me in on the latest trends and fads. And a very big thank-you to my witty colleagues, the other Five Wiseguys: Jeff Kent, Bob Lohbauer, Sam Bittman, and Matt Tannenbaum. They inspire mirth.

ABOUT THE AUTHOR

DANIEL KLEIN is the *New York Times*–bestselling co-author of *Plato and a Platypus Walk into a Bar* and the author of many other fiction, nonfiction, and humor titles. He lives in Great Barrington, Massachusetts.